Purple Ronnie's Guide to Girls

Also by Purple Ronnie

Purple Ronnie's Book of Love

☆

Purple Ronnie's Guide to Life

☆

The Smashing World of Purple Ronnie

☆

Purple Ronnie's Star Signs

☆

Purple Ronnie's Love Poems

☆

The Very Best of Purple Ronnie

☆

Purple Ronnie's Guide to Men

Published in 1997 by Statics (London) Ltd,
41 Standard Road, London NW10 6HF
Tel: 0181 965 3327

©1997 Purple Enterprises Ltd.

ISBN 1-873922-63-9

Print Origination by Diva Graphics

Printed in England by H.P.H. Print Ltd.
Unit 3, Royal London Estate, 29 North Acton Road
London NW10 6PE

Words by: Giles Andreae
Pictures by: Janet Cronin

Contents

1. Hippy Chicks

2. Girly Girls

3. Sex Goddesses

4. Posh Girls

5. Earth Mothers

6. Ladettes

7. Mumsy Girls

8. Sporty Girls

9. Bimbettes

10. Perfect Girls

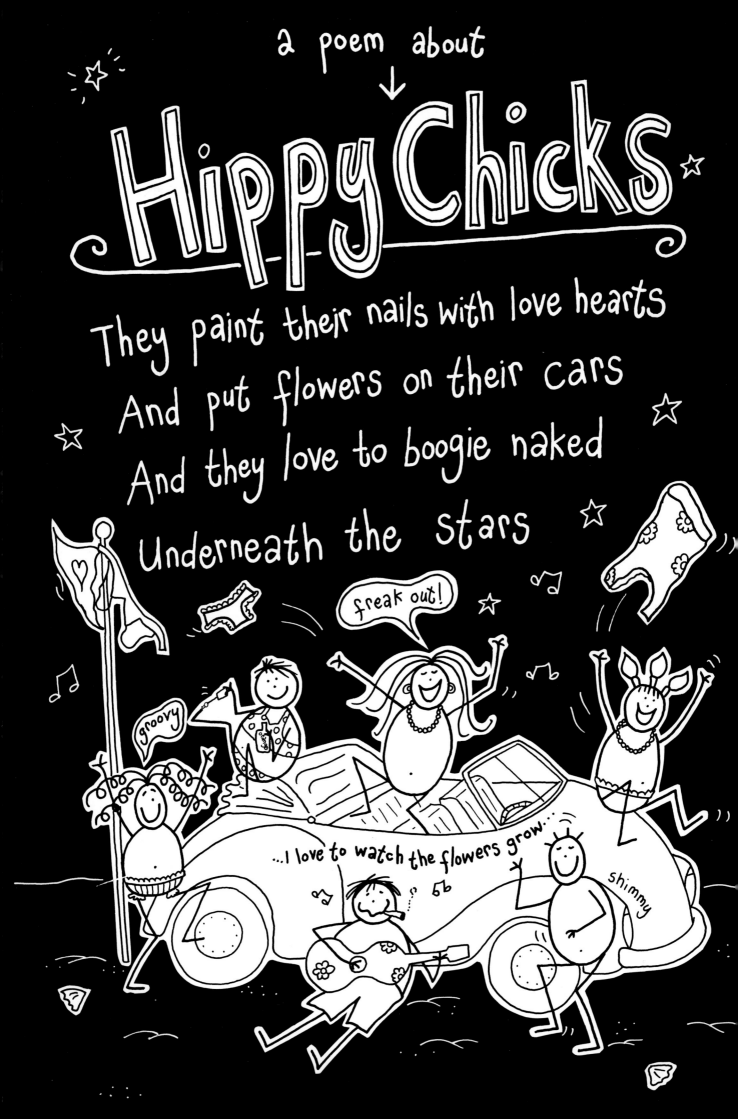

How to Spot a Hippy Chick

Looks

Hippy Chicks like to be unique. The last thing they want is to look like anyone else

Hippy Chicks have

Spacey Smiles

and

crazy hairstyles

Weave

Clothes Hippy Chicks wear

bright colourful clothes

dazzle

funky hats

and loads of ethnic jewellery

magic crystal

Hippy Chicks love buying funny clothes from charity shops

raggy cardie

← granny boots

that's 20p dear

old man's shoes →

What Are Hippy Chicks Like?

Character

Hippy Chicks are very groovy and they love to freak out and go crazy

A Hippy Chick is never frightened of saying exactly what she feels ♡

Friends

Hippy Chicks are great at making friends with all kinds of people

It is almost impossible to get Hippy Chicks in a bad mood

What Do Hippy Chicks Do?

Work

Hippy Chicks often earn their living from doing all sorts of arty stuff

Hobbies

Hippy Chicks love to spend their weekends shopping in markets

Interests

What Hippy Chicks like best is going on all sorts of adventurous travels

Hippy Chicks and Romance

Special Tip

The Moon always makes Hippy Chicks feel incredibly sexy

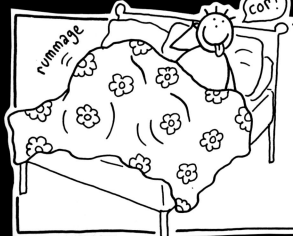

When they're in the mood Hippy Chicks are brilliant at Doing it and they love trying out all sorts of new tricks

There is nothing a Hippy Chick loves more than getting down to a good bit of body painting

Warning :-

If you want to go out with a Hippy Chick you must be prepared to share her with her guru

Chapter 2

GIRLY GIRLS

blush

a poem about Girly Girls

If you meet a Girly Girl
Just ask her for her name
And she'll end up all confused and in a muddle
Cos all that she knows how to do
Is giggle all the time
And give small fluffy animals a cuddle

How to Spot a Girly Girl

Looks

Girly Girls have long eyelashes, chubby cheeks and little button noses with freckles on them

They have masses of soft hair which they like to...

...twiddle round their fingers

... suck

...and put into bunches

Girly Girls always smell of roses

Clothes A Girly Girl's clothes are all decorated with either :-

Animals

or

flowers

What Are Girly Girls Like?

Character

There is one thing that Girly Girls do all the time. And that is GIGGLE

Girly Girls are very happy people who like to smile and skip and be fluffy

Friends

Girly Girls do not tend to make friends with people who like having deep conversations

A Girly Girl's best friend can often not talk at all

What Do Girly Girls Do?

Work

Girly Girls are always good at decorating things and making them look pretty

Hobbies

A Girly Girl's favourite hobby is going to the beauty parlour with her friends

Interests

There is nothing a Girly Girl loves more than watching a good weepy movie on the telly

Girly Girls and Romance

Girly Girls are amazing flirts and they know exactly how to get any man they want

Special Tip

A Girly Girl likes to do lots of talking about how much you love each other

Warning:-

Girly Girls don't really like Doing It. They think it's all a bit messy

Girly Girls always cry when they get married

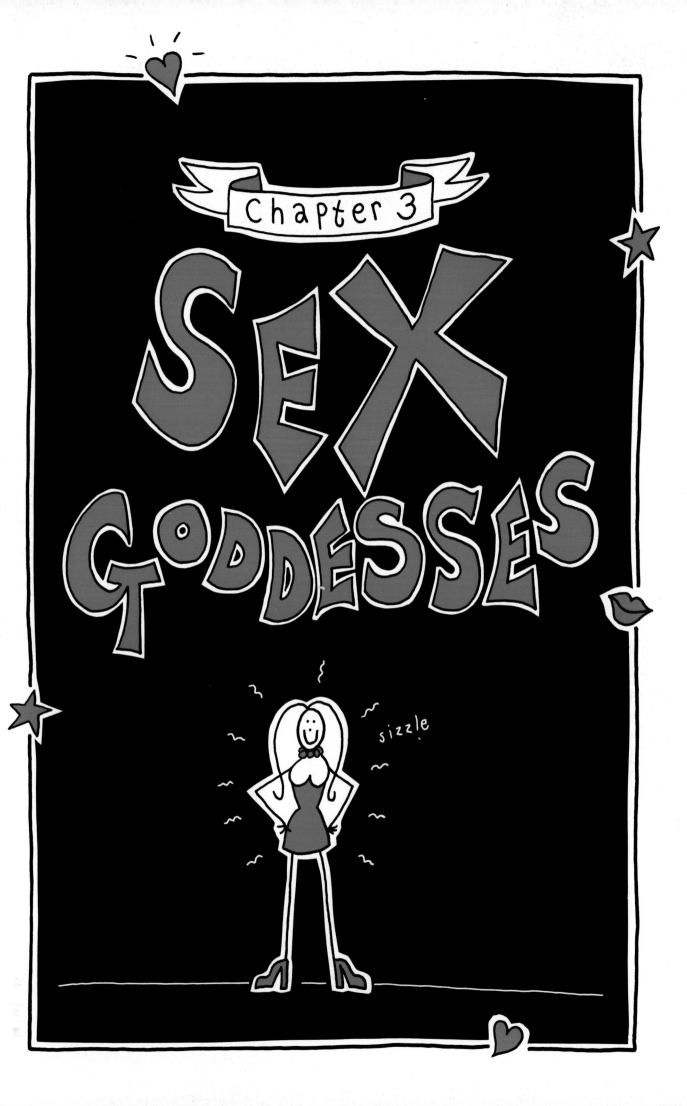

a poem about ↓

Sex Goddesses

They pout at themselves in the mirror
To get into Sex Goddess mode
Then wink at the boys who walk past them
And smile as their trousers explode

How to Spot a Sex Goddess

Looks

A Sex Goddess' body is enough to turn most grown-up men into dribbling babies

But as every woman knows, a body like that does not always come easily

Clothes

Sex Goddesses look best with no clothes on at all. But when they have to wear them, they like to show off their favourite bits

What Are Sex Goddesses Like?

Character

Sex Goddesses often try to talk about brainy things in case you only fancy them for their looks

The problem is that most Sex Goddesses have never had to use their brains so they have often turned to jelly

Friends

However nice a Sex Goddess is she can sometimes find it hard work to make friends with other girls

Sex Goddesses have lots of men friends who they think are just friends

What Do Sex Goddesses Do?

Work

Sex Goddesses are born to be actresses or movie stars

Hobbies

Sex Goddesses like to help their friends with their artistic projects

Interests

Sex Goddesses are interested in making the world a better place to live

Sex Goddesses and Romance

Lots of men are too frightened to date Sex Goddesses so they often end up with the kind of boyfriends you might not expect

Special Tip:-

Sex Goddesses always fall in love with men who make them laugh

Sex Goddesses like you to see their best bits close up

Warning :-

When you are Doing It with a Sex Goddess it is best to think of something completely different if you want it to last for more than 5 seconds

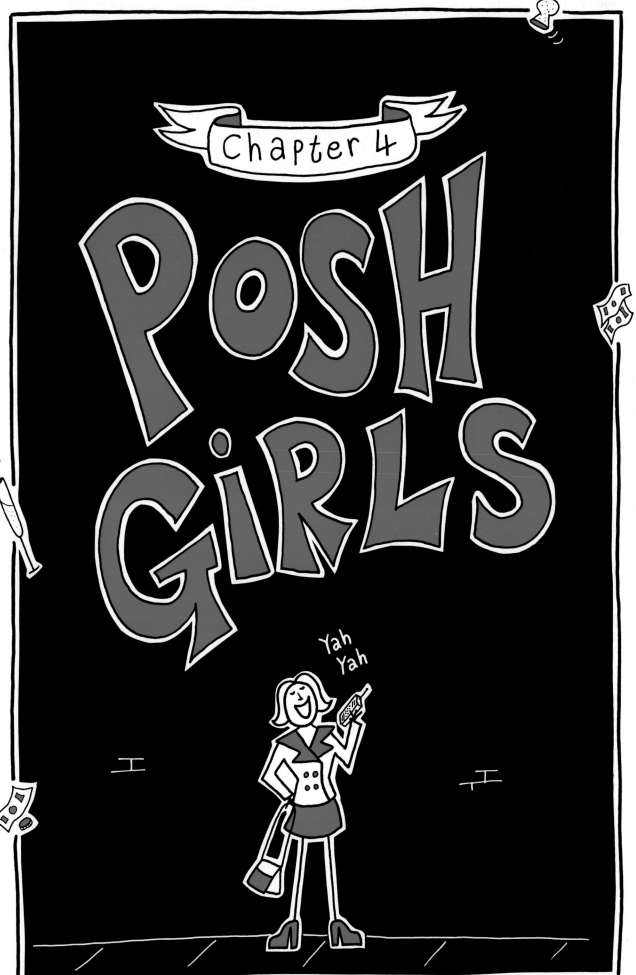

a poem about Posh Girls

No matter where they come from
They always talk the same
And they like to give each other
A very silly name

How to Spot a Posh Girl

Looks

Posh Girls walk around with their noses in the air as if everyone else smells a bit funny

Posh Girls' bodies are always very well looked after

Clothes

A Posh Girl loves to get her clothes made by very fancy designers

But they never think they've got the right thing to wear

What Are Posh Girls Like?

Character

Posh Girls can be very friendly but it is sometimes difficult to understand what they are saying

Posh Girls are often quite tough because they are taught by nuns in schools like prisons

Friends

A Posh Girl loves having her friends round for dinner parties

No-one has more friends than a Posh Girl

Work

Posh Girls don't really need jobs but they like to do their bit for charity

Hobbies

Posh Girls are very keen on weekends full of country pursuits

Interests

There is nothing a Posh Girl loves more than having lunch with friends and swapping shopping tips

Posh Girls and Romance

f you want to date a Posh Girl, first you have to get past her Dad

Special Tip:-
Posh Girl's love to have some rumpy-pumpy with a bit of rough

Posh Girls are not afraid to tell you what to do in bed and they are often quite demanding

Warning:-
Posh Girls can sometimes have some rather

Chapter 5

EARTH MOTHERS

right on

Earth Mothers

They love having baths in rhinoceros dung
And rubbing their bosoms with clay
It may not look pretty
Or smell very nice
But it's just much more natural that way

How to Spot an Earth Mother

Looks

Earth Mothers believe they should look the way nature intended them to look

earthy waft

hairy legs

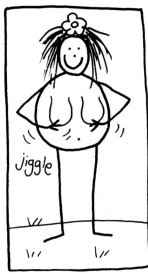

jiggle

Earth Mothers like everything to hang loose especially their bosoms, which they can often tie together behind their backs

tug

tie

Clothes

Earth Mothers think clothes are for people who are ashamed of their bodies. But when they have to wear them, they like :-

smashing

spin

weave

itch

1. Baggy scratchy things made from plants

baah!

skip

v. cosy

2. Woolly things made from very happy sheep

What Are Earth Mothers Like?

Character

Earth Mothers like to find all sorts of ways to achieve relaxation and inner peace

Friends

Anyone who is a friend of the world is a friend of an Earth Mother

Earth Mothers love to bond with their friends

Earth Mothers like to call their best friends "Sister"

What Do Earth Mothers Do?

Work

Earth Mothers do not need jobs because they can grow everything they need at home

Hobbies

Earth Mothers spend their spare time going on marches and protests

Interests

Earth Mothers are very into alternative healing

Earth Mothers and Romance

Earth Mothers prefer romantic camping holidays to expensive weekends at posh hotels

Special Tip
Nothing turns an Earth Mother on more than a good sniff of your armpits

Warning :- It is a good idea to wear ear plugs when you are Doing It with an Earth Mother

Earth Mothers make great lovers because they are so in touch with their bodies

Chapter 6

LADETTES

cheers!

a poem about
Ladettes

Dating Ladettes is quite frightening

Because they are easily able

To gobble hot curries

Drink twenty-five pints

And then nail your knob to the table

How to Spot a Ladette

Looks

The easiest way to spot a Ladette is to look for:-

A. Body Piercing

B. Tattoos

They often have short hair and like to sit with their legs wide open

Clothes

Ladettes love wearing tight T-shirts and jeans to show off their figures

Dresses are girly

what Ladettes think

Pants are for wimps

What Are Ladettes Like?

Character

Ladettes get their thrills from doing anything that is dangerous or daring

Ladettes are loud and confident, and they often like to shock people in public

Friends

Ladettes believe in Girl Power, and they think most men are boring

All Ladettes like to have a good laugh

Work

Ladettes are often Pop Stars or T.V. presenters because they love showing off

Hobbies

A Ladette loves nothing more than getting together with her mates for a good session down the pub

Interests

Ladettes are mad about sport, especially football and they have crushes on lots of football players

Ladettes and Romance

Ladettes are not very romantic and they like to be up-front about what's going on

Special Tip:-
Ladettes always love Doing It in interesting places

Do not be surprised if a Ladette asks you personal questions

Warning :-
Ladettes like to tell you all about every other person they've slept with

Chapter 7

MUMSY GIRLS

stride

a poem about ↓

MUMSY Girls

It's best to avoid them in public

Cos if you sneak off to the lav

They shout at you

"please wipe your bottom

And don't come back here till you have"

How to Spot a Mumsy Girl

Looks

Mumsy Girls have short straight hair which they make a little bit curly at the ends when they go out to the shops

Mumsy Girls often have giant bosoms which they are always shifting around

Clothes

Mumsy Girls prefer sensible clothes to clothes that make them look good

Mumsy Girls always have the right clothes for the weather

What Are Mumsy Girls Like?

Character

A Mumsy Girl has an opinion on everything and she always thinks she knows what's best for everyone

Mumsy Girls are obsessed with keeping their houses clean and tidy

Friends

If you've got a problem there is no better friend to share it with than a Mumsy Girl

What Do Mumsy Girls Do?

Work

Mumsy Girls are very good at any job that involves organising people

Hobbies

Mumsy Girls like to get into a good bit of knitting or tapestry

Interests

There is nothing a Mumsy Girl loves more than a breath of fresh air in the great outdoors

Mumsy Girls and Romance

Mumsy Girls are not shy about anything and they like to get down to business in a matter-of-fact way

Mumsy Girls love to spank naughty little boys

Special Tip:- Do not ask a Mumsy Girl out if you don't want to get married on your first date

Warning:-

Mumsy Girls love Doing It so they can make babies

Chapter 8

SPORTY GIRLS

Yeah!

a poem about Sporty Girls

It's best to tell a Sporty Girl
That she's the one for you
Cos if you don't
She'll grab your wrist
And break your arm in two

How to Spot a Sporty Girl

Looks

Sporty Girls' bodies are firm and toned and ready for action

extra firm botty muscles ↓

spring

special sporty bra →

no wobbling ←

boring!

jog

Sporty Girls strap their bosoms to their chests with special bras that stop them bouncing around

Clothes

A Sporty Girl has a different pair of trainers for every occasion

?

BOOGYING | SLOBBING
WATCHING T.V. | PULLING
PLAYING | GETTING PISSED

up the crack ←

When Sporty Girls go to the gym they wear outfits that make them look completely naked

What Are Sporty Girls Like?

Character

Sporty Girls are fun and bouncy and full of energy

But they can sometimes be a bit one-track minded

Friends

When you are introduced to a sporty Girl it is best not to shake her hand

Sporty Girls like to make everything they do into a competition

What Do Sporty Girls Do?

Work

Sporty Girls like to make sure that everyone keeps fit and healthy

Hobbies

Being a Sporty Girl is a way of life. There is no time for other hobbies

Interests

What Sporty Girls are interested in most is measuring what their bodies are up to all the time

Sporty Girls and Romance

Sporty Girls are so fit that it usually only takes one drink to get them completely pissed

Warning:- When it comes to Doing It, Sporty Girls love to give you a full work-out

Special Tip:-

It is best not to let a Sporty Girl see you naked until she is completely in love with you

Sporty Girls can be very handy people to go out with

BIMBETTES

a poem about Bimbettes

They love to go shopping together
And spend all the money they have
At night they just dance round their handbags

And laugh about boys in the Lav

How to Spot a Bimbette

Looks

Bimbettes have big teeth, big lips, big bosoms and big hair

They also have a year-round orange tan which they get from bottles and machines

Clothes

Bimbettes love make-up, handbags, high heels and strappy shoes

On the beach Bimbettes wear bikinis made from little bits of string

What Are Bimbettes Like?

Character

Bimbettes love to have a good time, but they can often be a bit noisy

Bimbettes can sometimes be bitchy...

... but usually they have hearts of gold

Friends

Bimbettes make very good friends - especially if you like to gossip

What Do Bimbettes Do?

Work

Bimbettes are always very good at selling things

Hobbies

There is nothing a Bimbette loves more than a good night out with the girls

Interests

Bimbettes are very interested in all the latest hairdressing techniques

Bimbettes and Romance

A Bimbette always loves to be treated like a lady

Special Tip:-
It is essential to give a Bimbette loads of fancy cocktails if you want to snog her

Warning :-
Bimbettes go sex crazy on holiday, and try to Do It with anyone in sight

When you kiss a Bimbette they always taste of lipstick, perfume and make-up

Chapter 10

PERFECT GIRLS

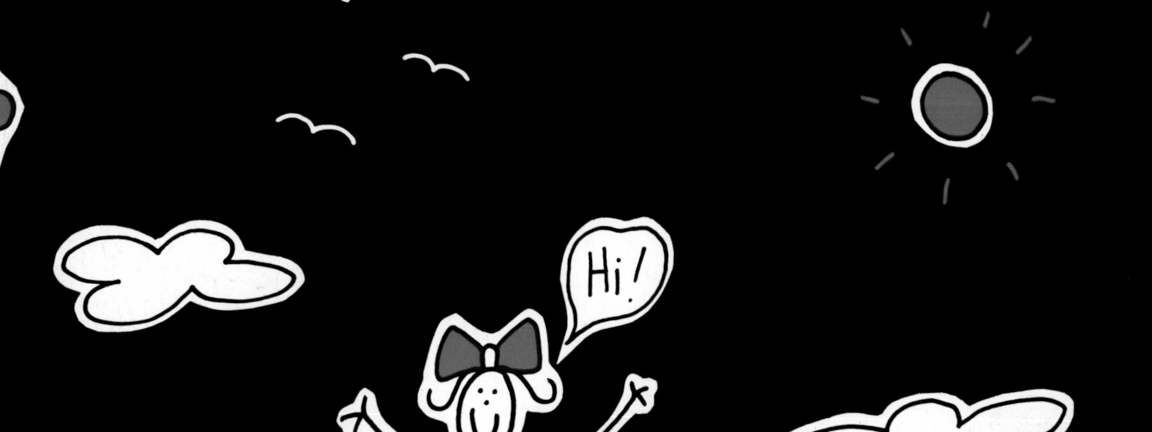

a poem about Perfect Girls

You may think I'm being soft-headed

You may think I'm being a fool

But I would call any girl perfect

Who tells me I'm sexy and cool

How to Spot a Perfect Girl

Looks

Ideally a Perfect Girl's body is neither too fat

...nor too thin

But really, a Perfect Girl's body is fantastic if <u>she</u> likes it, whatever it looks like

↑   ↗

see what
← I mean ?

Clothes

What Are Perfect Girls Like?

Character

Perfect Girls think that life is smashing and they always have a good time... whatever

Even your Mum loves a Perfect Girl

Friends

Perfect Girls think all your friends are smashing and that you should spend lots of time with them

Perfect Girls have some pretty smashing friends of their own as well

What Do Perfect Girls Do?

Work

Perfect Girls have jobs that give you lots of free holidays

Hobbies

Perfect Girls think that your hobbies are very interesting and great fun

Interests

A Perfect Girl is interested in equal rights for everyone

Perfect Girls and Romance

Perfect Girls never had any other boyfriend who meant anything to them

When a Perfect Girl kisses you for the first time your whole body wants to explode with happiness

When you take off your clothes Perfect Girls know exactly what to say...

...and exactly what to do

Special Tip:—

Perfect Girls make you feel like this feeling's never going to end